21st Century Junior Library

Respect

by Lucia Raatma

CHERRY LAKE PUBLISHING * ANN ARBOR, MICHIGAN

CHERRY LAKE
Publishing

Published in the United States of America by Cherry Lake Publishing
Ann Arbor, Michigan
www.cherrylakepublishing.com

Content Adviser: David Wangaard, Executive Director, SEE: The School for Ethical Education, Milford, Connecticut

Reading Adviser: Marla Conn, ReadAbility, Inc.

Photo Credits: Cover, ©lofoto/Dreamstime.com; page 4, ©Khakimullin Aleksandr/Shutterstock, Inc.; page 6, ©iStockphoto.com/aabejon; page 8, ©iStockphoto.com/jackscoldsweat; page 10, ©iStockphoto.com/Jbryson; page 12, ©Jacek Chabraszewski/Dreamstime.com; page 14, ©Pressmaster/Shutterstock, Inc.; page 16, ©margouillat photo/Shutterstock, Inc.; page 18, ©Morgan Lane Photography/Shutterstock, Inc.; page 20, ©Jhdt Stock Images Llc/Dreamstime.com.

LIBRARY OF CONGRESS CATALOGING-IN-PUBLICATION DATA
Raatma, Lucia.
 Respect/by Lucia Raatma.
     pages cm.—(Character education) (21st century junior library)
 Includes bibliographical references and index.
 ISBN 978-1-62431-156-7 (lib. bdg.)—ISBN 978-1-62431-222-9 (e-book)—
ISBN 978-1-62431-288-5 (pbk.)
 1. Respect—Juvenile literature. I. Title.
BJ1533.R4R33 2013
177'.1—dc23   2013004930

Cherry Lake Publishing would like to acknowledge the work of
The Partnership for 21st Century Skills.
Please visit www.p21.org *for more information.*

Printed in the United States of America
Corporate Graphics Inc.
July 2013
CLFA13

CONTENTS

Talking in a movie theater is disrespectful to the other people in the audience.

What Is Respect?

Rob and Jason were watching a movie at the theater. Rob loudly made a joke about the movie.

"Be quiet!" Jason shouted as he threw a piece of popcorn at Rob. The two boys noticed as a few people turned around to look at them.

"We should probably be quieter," Rob whispered. "It's not very respectful to ruin the movie for everyone."

It is disrespectful to talk about someone
behind his back.

Respect is treating others the way you would like to be treated. It also means thinking about other people's feelings. You don't show respect when you **insult** or make fun of others.

Respectful people are polite. They listen to other people. They get to know people before making **judgments** about them.

Think!

Remember a time when someone was rude to you or teased you. How did it make you feel? Would you ever want to make someone else feel that way?

Show respect for your parents by following the rules they make.

Showing Respect

There are many ways to show respect at home. Andy follows his parents' rules. He does not make a mess that his parents will have to clean up. He doesn't yell and run through the house. He is nice to his brothers and sisters.

Marvin is respectful of other people's things. He asks before taking or borrowing something. He is also careful not to break things that are important to other people.

Your teachers work hard to help you learn. Show respect by listening to what they say.

At school, you should respect your teachers. Chris pays attention to the things they teach him. He is always sure to follow classroom rules.

Michelle always shows respect to her classmates. She does not talk when they are talking. She doesn't make fun of the things they say.

Create!

Make a list of people you respect and look up to. It might include parents, teachers, or other people who have helped you. Share the list with your parents or an adult you trust. Talk about why you respect the people on the list.

You can show respect for your friends by listening to their problems.

Juan shows respect for his friends. He does not say hurtful things to them. He shares his things with them and invites them to play at his house. Juan also respects his friends by helping with their problems. He listens to what they have to say. He tries to give them good advice.

You should respect the beliefs and lifestyles of people from all around the world.

Respecting Your World

It is important to treat everyone with respect. When Marcus meets new people, he tries not to judge them. Sometimes people feel uneasy around people who are different. Marcus takes the time to learn about new people, and different **cultures** and ideas.

You can show respect for your neighbors by offering to help take care of their pets.

You can show respect in your neighborhood by treating others well. You should never play tricks on your neighbors. Damaging other people's homes or yards is not showing respect.

Wendy offers to bring in her neighbor's newspaper each day. She also offers to walk or feed another neighbor's dog. They are happy she helped!

Recycling helps show respect for our planet.

Another way to be respectful is to take care of the **environment**. Brandon shows respect by not littering or wasting water. Kiki shows respect by **recycling** bottles, cans, and paper. Choose to keep Earth healthy. Your efforts will **benefit** people now. You will also be helping keep Earth clean for future people!

Your friends will respect you if you respect them.

When you show respect, your friendships with other people can become stronger. Your family will know that you care about them. The way you treat others can make a difference in their lives. They will treat you with respect, too!

Look!

Watch the people around you. Notice how your neighbors talk to one another. See how kids you know treat their friends. Do they show respect? How could they be more respectful? Share your ideas with your parents or friends.

GLOSSARY

benefit (BEN-uh-fit) to be useful or helpful to someone or something

cultures (KUHL-churz) the ideas, customs, and traditions of different groups of people

environment (en-VYE-ruhn-muhnt) the world around you, including the land, sea, and air

insult (in-SUHLT) to say or do something rude or upsetting to others

judgments (JUHJ-muhnts) opinions about someone or something

recycling (ree-SYE-kuhl-ing) processing old items so they can be used to make new products

FIND OUT MORE

BOOKS

Kroll, Virginia L. *Ryan Respects*. Morton Grove, IL: Albert Whitman & Company, 2006.

Suen, Anastasia. *Show Some Respect*. Edina, MN: Magic Wagon, 2008.

WEB SITES

Respect—A Way of Life
www.cyh.sa.gov.au/HealthTopics /HealthTopicDetailsKids .aspx?p=335&np=287&id=2356
Read more about respecting yourself and others.

Whootie Owl's Stories
www.storiestogrowby.com/choose .php
Find folktales and fairy tales about respect and other good character traits.

INDEX

ABOUT THE AUTHOR

Lucia Raatma has written dozens of books for young readers. They are about famous people, historical events, ways to stay safe, and other topics. She lives in Florida's Tampa Bay area with her husband and their two children.